เรื่องเล่าของตัวเลข

THE NUMBER STORY

SMALL BOOK ONE

ENGLISH - THAI

Numbers Teach Children Their Number Names

written and illustrated by

MISS ANNA

Early Reader Edition of *The Number Story 1*
Bronze Medal Winner, 2016 Wishing Shelf Book Award

Library of Congress Control Number: 2018902040

Names: Miss Anna, author.
Title: Number story : numbers teach children their number names / Miss Anna.
Description: Portland, OR: Lumpy Publishing, 2018.
Identifiers: ISBN 978-1-945977-32-9 | LCCN 2018902040
Summary: The pictures and rhymes present stories which introduce numbers 0-10.
Subjects: LCSH Numeration—English--Thai--Pictorial works--Juvenile literature. | BISAC JUVENILE NONFICTION /
Languages: English--Thai
Classification: LCC QA141.3 .M57 2018 | DDC 513—dc23

Publisher: Lumpy Publishing
Website: www.missannabooks.com
Email: missanna@missannabooks.com

Paperback: ISBN 978-1-945977-32-9
Printed in the U.S.A.   1 3 5 7 9 10 8 6 4 2

อยากรู้ชื่อของตัวเลขต่างๆมั้ย?

It is very easy and a lot of fun!

มันง่ายและสนุกมากๆเลยนะ!

Say-along our little jingle

พูดตามไปพร้อมเสียงเพลงของพวกเรา

starting from Number One!
เรามาเริ่มกันที่เลขหนึ่ง!

1

ดูคล้ายกับนิ้วมือหนึ่งของฉัน

ONE!
หนึ่ง!

2
TWO   trails a tail.
๒ ✦ สอง
ลองเดินตามรอยหาง

หาง!

3

THREE has bumps.

๓ สาม
ดูเหมือนเนินเขา

ดูเนินเขาสีเขียวนั่นสิ!

4

FOUR carries a sail.

๔ สี่

คือเรือใบ

4
A SAIL!
เรือใบ!

5

FIVE   is a racing track.

๕ ★ ห้า

คือ สนามแข่ง

VROOM
บรี๊นนน!

6

SIX   curves like a snail.

๖ ✩ หก

มีรูปร่างคล้ายหอยทาก

รูปร่างคล้ายหอยทาก

A SNAIL! หอยทาก!

7
SEVEN has a sharp angle.
๗ เจ็ด
มีมุมแหลมเฟี้ยว

OUCH!
โอ๊ย!

8

EIGHT is rollercoaster rails.

๘ • แปด

คือรางรถไฟเหาะ

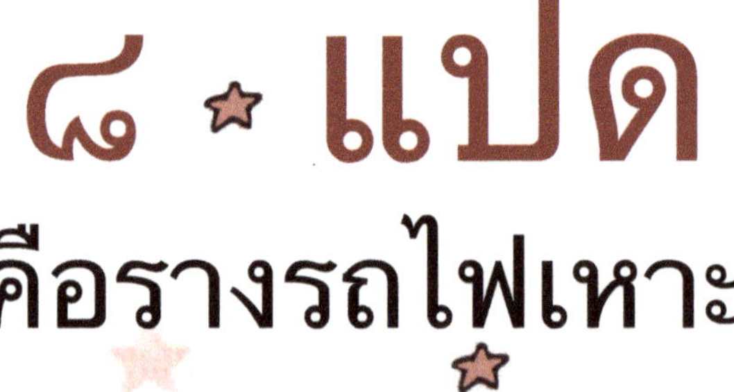

เย้!
YIPPEE!

NINE   is a bubble on a stick.

๙ เก้า

คือเล่นเป่าฟอง

A BUBBLE! ฟองสบู่!

10

TEN is an eye of a whale.

๑๐ สิบ

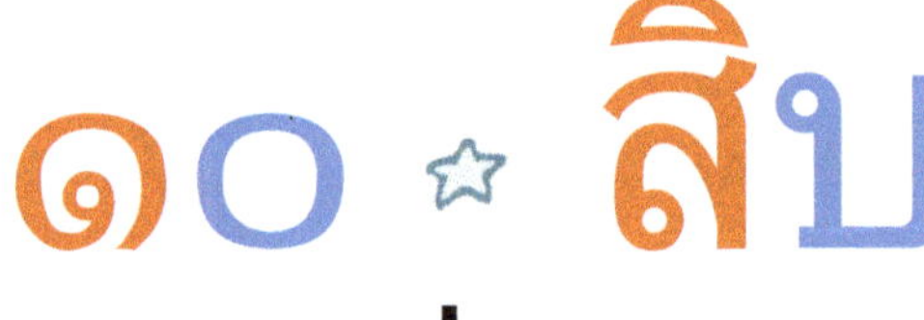

คือตาข้างหนึ่งของปลาวาฬ

ขยิบตา!
WINK!
HELLO! สวัสดี!

And
และ
0
ZERO   is an empty pail.

๐
ศูนย์
คือถังที่ว่างเปล่า

IT'S EMPTY!
มันว่างเปล่า!

Thank you for playing with us today.

We had a lot of fun too!

ขอบคุณที่ร่วมเล่นกับเราในวันนี้

เราสนุกกันมากเลย!

We are your Number friends,
Zero to Ten,
Who will be here for you~
เราเป็นเพื่อนของเธอ
จากศูนย์ถึงสิบ
เราจะอยู่ที่นี่เพื่อเธอ!

Bye-bye now!
See you again soon.
ลาก่อน!
แล้วพบกันใหม่!

The Numbers are *SINGING* too!

To sing-a-long, look for Miss Anna Number Story
at your favorite music store like iTUNES.

MP3

Numbers 0-10 IDENTIFYING & COUNTING	Numbers 11-20 & Ordinals first, second, third...	Numbers 0-100 & Place Values ones, tens, hundreds...	About Clocks & Telling Time hours, minutes, seconds

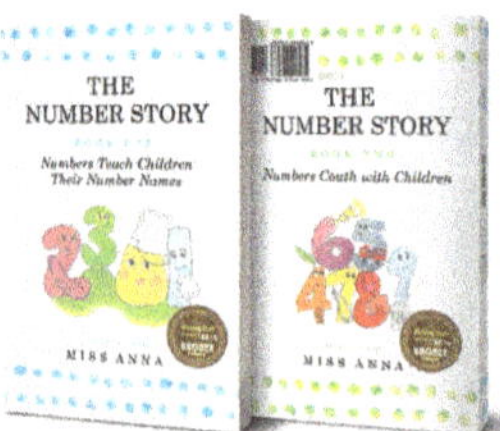   

Number Story 1 & 2

isbn: 978-0-996216-48-7

Number Story 3 & 4

isbn: 978-1-945977-01-5

Number Story 5 & 6

isbn: 978-1-945977-06-0

Number Story 7 & 8

isbn: 978-1-949320-40-4

For more Miss Anna books to love,
visit us at

www.missannabooks.com

Numbers are working hard all over the world!
Come Travel the World with Us!